DOOMED HISTORY

SURPRISE ATTACK!

Pearl Harbor, 1941

by Tim Cooke

BEARPORT
PUBLISHING

Minneapolis, Minnesota

Bearport Publishing Company Product Development Team
President: Jen Jenson; Director of Product Development: Spencer Brinker; Senior Editor: Allison Juda; Editor: Charly Haley; Associate Editor: Naomi Reich; Senior Designer: Colin O'Dea; Associate Designer: Elena Klinkner; Associate Designer: Kayla Eggert; Product Development Assistant: Anita Stasson

Brown Bear Books
Children's Publisher: Anne O'Daly; Design Manager: Keith Davis; Picture Manager: Sophie Mortimer

Library of Congress Cataloging-in-Publication Data

Names: Cooke, Tim, 1961- author.
Title: Surprise attack! : Pearl Harbor, 1941 / by Tim Cooke.
Other titles: Pearl Harbor, 1941
Description: Minneapolis, Minnesota : Bearport Publishing, 2023. | Series: Doomed history | Includes bibliographical references and index.
Identifiers: LCCN 2022046631 (print) | LCCN 2022046632 (ebook) | ISBN 9798885093989 (library binding) | ISBN 9798885095204 (paperback) | ISBN 9798885096355 (ebook)
Subjects: LCSH: Pearl Harbor (Hawaii), Attack on, 1941--Juvenile literature.
Classification: LCC D767.92 .C665 2023 (print) | LCC D767.92 (ebook) | DDC 940.54/26693--dc23/eng/20220928
LC record available at https://lccn.loc.gov/2022046631
LC ebook record available at https://lccn.loc.gov/2022046632

For more information, write to Bearport Publishing, 5357 Penn Avenue South, Minneapolis, MN 55419.

CONTENTS

Surprise Attack 4

The First Signs of Danger 6

Disaster Strikes........................... 12

Life or Death 20

What Happened Next 26

Key Dates 30
Quiz...30
Glossary..31
Index...32
Read More 32
Learn More Online....................................32

SURPRISE ATTACK

As World War II (1939—1945) began, the United States stayed out of the fighting. But that changed after December 7, 1941, when a surprise attack hit Pearl Harbor.

It was a sunny Sunday morning. Many of the 18,000 U.S. Navy and Army **personnel** stationed on the Hawaiian Island of Oahu were looking forward to a day off. Pearl Harbor was home to the U.S. Pacific Fleet of almost 100 navy vessels, including 8 **battleships**. Hundreds of aircraft were also based on the island.

An aerial view shows U.S. ships in Pearl Harbor before the attack.

Smoke rises from the destroyer USS *Shaw* after a direct hit by a Japanese bomber.

Going to War

Suddenly, more than 350 Japanese fighter planes and bombers filled the sky. The attack killed 2,403 U.S. servicemen and **civilians**. It left more than a dozen ships destroyed or badly damaged. The next day, U.S. President Franklin D. Roosevelt called on Congress to vote to join the war against the **Axis powers** of Germany, Italy, and Japan.

THE FIRST SIGN OF DANGER

For years before the attack, Japan had been gaining power in the Pacific region. As the country's strength grew, its relationship with the United States became strained.

In the 1880s, Japan began to rapidly build up industry. At the same time, it created a strong army and navy. The country wanted to become a world power, but in order to do so, it needed **resources**. Japan's leaders decided to gain access to more coal, rubber, and oil by taking control of Southeast Asia.

Japan was prepared to use force to gain resources and power.

Spreading Control

In 1937, Japan invaded China, launching a full-scale war between the countries. Meanwhile, a different war was beginning to take shape. World War II pulled Europe's focus away from the region then known as Indochina and toward fighting on their own continent. Japan took advantage of the distraction and pushed into the territory.

INDOCHINA

The region of Indochina spread across present-day Laos, Cambodia, and Vietnam. The area had been ruled by France since the late 1800s. After the start of World War II in 1939, France was fighting Germany in Europe, so it could no longer defend Indochina.

Sending a Message

In response to Japan's aggression at the start of the war, President Roosevelt stopped selling military-related goods to Japan. He ordered the U.S. Pacific Fleet to move from California to Hawaii. Then, Japan signed a **pact** with Germany and Italy, agreeing to fight together if any of the countries were attacked. Though the United States was not yet in the war, Japan hoped the new pact would send a clear message: leave Japan alone.

The Pearl Harbor attack was planned by the commander of the Japanese fleet, Admiral Isoroku Yamamoto.

Plan of Attack

Tension between Japan and the United States grew as the Americans were denying Japan key resources it needed. Most importantly, Japan struggled to find enough oil for the tanks and warplanes it used in its continued **expansion** in Southeast Asia. So, Japan's military leaders began planning a response. They designed an attack that would destroy the U.S. Pacific Fleet.

EMPEROR HIROHITO

Japan's Emperor Hirohito was hesitant to go to war with China or the United States. But the Japanese military leaders overruled him.

In the 1920s, Japan had built the world's first aircraft carrier, the *Hosho*.

Moving In

Throughout the fall of 1941, Japanese and U.S. leaders tried to discuss a resolution. President Roosevelt said he would sell goods to Japan again if they agreed to withdraw from Indochina. Even as the talks progressed, the Japanese military began to move **aircraft carriers** and other ships toward Hawaii.

NAVAL PLANNER

The attack on Pearl Harbor was planned by Admiral Isoroku Yamamoto, who had studied at Harvard University and greatly admired the United States. Yamamoto believed wars could only be won by air power, so he ordered warplanes to be built. He died in 1943 when his own airplane was shot down by U.S. forces.

The Emperor's Message

Pearl Harbor is 4,000 miles (6,400 km) from Japan. U.S. military leaders thought this was far enough away to keep it safe from attack. But now, 30 hidden Japanese ships and **submarines**—including 6 aircraft carriers with hundreds of warplanes—gathered 230 miles (370 km) north of Hawaii. In Japan, Emperor Hirohito met with his military commanders, who argued Japan had to strike first to gain an advantage. On December 2, 1941, the emperor sent a coded message to the commanders: Climb Mt. Niitaka. The attack was on.

Mount Niitaka in Taiwan was once the tallest mountain in the Japanese empire.

DISASTER STRIKES

The seas in the Pacific were rough as the Japanese military prepared to launch an attack on Pearl Harbor.

Japanese aircraft carriers rolled in the waves. The crew had to hang onto the planes to stop them from sliding off the decks. Still, they moved forward with their plans. A Japanese submarine headed toward the harbor. Just after 6:00 a.m., Japanese commander Mitsuo Fuchida ordered the first wave of airplanes to take off. One after another, they took to the skies until 183 planes were airborne.

Sailors cheered as bombers took off from the carriers.

The Japanese military planned to use submarines to attack U.S. warships docked at Pearl Harbor.

First Shots

At 6:45 a.m., crew members on a U.S. **patrol boat** near the entrance to Pearl Harbor spotted something in the water. When they realized it was an enemy submarine trying to get into the harbor, the crew fired their guns and set off underwater bombs to blow it up. These were the first shots fired by the United States in World War II.

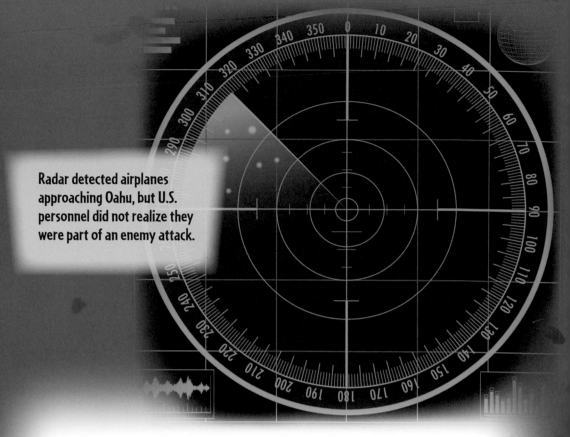

Radar detected airplanes approaching Oahu, but U.S. personnel did not realize they were part of an enemy attack.

Another Sign

Meanwhile, on the northern tip of Oahu, two U.S. airmen kept watch at a **radar** station. Suddenly, the screen lit up, showing a group of at least 50 airplanes only 140 miles (220 km) away. The airmen reported what they saw, but an army lieutenant told them not to worry. A group of U.S. planes was expected to arrive from California, so the lieutenant thought that was what had shown up on the radar. No warning was sent out.

AIRCRAFT CARRIERS

The Japanese hoped to destroy the aircraft carriers of the U.S. Pacific Fleet to make it harder for the United States to fight back in the Pacific. On the day of the attack, however, the U.S. carriers were out at sea.

The Second Wave

By 7:30 a.m., a second wave of Japanese warplanes was in the skies, and a total of 353 planes were now heading for Pearl Harbor. Fuchida led the first wave of pilots toward their target. As they neared, clouds above the island lifted. The Japanese could see the U.S. battleships ahead. Everything was on track for the attack.

A Japanese aircraft carrying a bomb beneath its wings takes off from a carrier deck.

Bombs that did not hit their targeted ships sent water spraying high into the sky.

Attack!

The secret plan had worked. By the time the Americans finally noticed the Japanese approaching, it was too late for them to pull together their defenses. At 7:49 a.m., Fuchida gave the official order to attack. While **torpedo** bomber planes flew toward the American battleships sitting in the harbor, other aircraft headed toward four airfields on the island.

AN EASY TARGET

Ships in the Pacific Fleet were docked close together in the harbor. Eight battleships sat side by side along what was called Battleship Row. This made them easy targets for Japanese pilots. Similarly, in the airfields on Oahu, U.S. airplanes were parked close together.

Sleepy Sunday Morning

Sundays at Pearl Harbor meant a day off for most U.S. personnel. When people first noticed fighter planes flying overhead at about 7:55 a.m., they thought U.S. pilots were practicing. Even when bombs started to fall, people were slow to realize an attack had begun. It was only when they saw red circles—the national symbol of Japan—on the wings of the planes that they understood enemy forces had invaded.

Admiral Husband E. Kimmel (center) was commander of the Pacific Fleet at the time of the attack.

This Is No Drill

Admiral Kimmel, the U.S. commander of Pearl Harbor, was home when the attack began. As thick smoke began to rise from ships in the harbor, he realized they were under attack. At 8:00 a.m., he radioed his forces, declaring the harbor was being attacked.

Waves of Japanese bombers continued to approach Battleship Row, even as ships there were already on fire.

The USS *West Virginia* sunk in the attack but was later recovered.

Panic!

Over the next 15 minutes, Pearl Harbor was a scene of panic. Bomb after bomb exploded, killing many sailors as they tried to fight back. Injured sailors took over the ships' guns as their fellows died. Below deck, men became trapped in flooded rooms as water gushed through holes made by the bombs. Fires raged and black smoke rose into the sky. Still, Japanese planes continued to bomb the harbor.

LIFE OR DEATH

In just 15 minutes, the Japanese attack caused unbelievable damage and loss of life. Caught by surprise, U.S. personnel kept trying to fight back.

At 8:05 a.m. the battleship USS *Oklahoma* was hit by the first of seven torpedoes. Seawater poured into holes in its **hull,** and it rolled onto its side. Just eight minutes later, the ship sank. Those who could jumped 50 feet (15 m) into the sea. But more than 400 people were trapped and died in the sinking vessel.

USS *Oklahoma* rolled on its side as it sank, trapping hundreds of its crew members inside.

The Horror Continues

The docked battleships continued to be attacked.
After the *Oklahoma* was hit, torpedoes blasted
USS *West Virginia* and USS *Utah*. The pride of the
U.S. Navy was being destroyed. At the same time,
Japanese pilots were also bombing American
planes parked at inland airfields.

A DECLARATION OF WAR

The Japanese had intended to declare war
on the United States before the attack on
Pearl Harbor. But Japanese **diplomats** in
Washington, D.C., were slow to deliver the
message to American officials. War was not
officially declared until almost an hour
and a half after the attack had begun.

USS *Arizona* was one of the most powerful battleships in the Pacific Fleet.

USS *Arizona*

At 600 ft (180 m) long and with a crew of 1,500, the battleship USS Arizona was like a small floating town. Its decks were covered with thick **armor**, so it was able to survive the first torpedo attacks. But then, a Japanese plane dropped a bomb from high above. The bomb hit the deck with such force that it pierced the armor and blew up the ammunition stored below. As more than 1 million pounds (450,000 kg) of **gunpowder** ignited, the ship exploded, killing 1,177 people.

FAMILY TRAGEDIES

Many sailors on USS *Arizona* were brothers who were serving alongside each other. So many brothers died onboard that the U.S. Navy changed its rules to no longer allow siblings to serve on the same ship.

Death of a Ship

The force of the blast lifted the battleship several feet into the air. Flames shot into the sky as sailors were thrown from the ship. The *Arizona* suddenly broke in two, sending shock waves across the island. The explosion was so strong that it knocked sailors off other ships docked nearby.

The *Arizona* sank after it exploded.

DECEMBER 7th 1941 — REMEMBER!!

Sailor Dorie Miller was awarded the Navy Cross for firing back at the Japanese airplanes.

A Sea of Fire

Pearl Harbor was a scene of fiery destruction. The damaged ships were leaking oil, which then caught fire even as it pooled in the sea. Inland, the attacked airfields also burned. The bombing continued until the Japanese pilots had used all their ammunition. At 8:35 a.m., the Japanese planes turned away. But the attack was not over.

JAPANESE WARPLANES

The Japanese used fighter planes and bombers in the attack. Their fighter planes moved faster than U.S. planes. From high up in the air, bombers dropped torpedoes made specially for Pearl Harbor's shallow waters.

A Second Wave

About 20 minutes later, the second wave of 170 Japanese bombers approached Pearl Harbor. But this time, the U.S. sailors were more organized and were prepared to fight back. Sailors manned the guns on the ships that were still floating. They shot down several Japanese planes. However, they could not stop every plane headed their way. At 9:30 a.m. USS *Shaw* exploded.

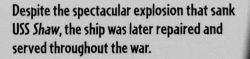

Despite the spectacular explosion that sank USS *Shaw*, the ship was later repaired and served throughout the war.

WHAT HAPPENED NEXT

The attack on Pearl Harbor lasted for two hours. It left thousands dead and the U.S. Pacific Fleet almost completely destroyed.

Japan had lost 29 airplanes and 64 pilots. Meanwhile, 2,403 Americans had been killed, including 68 civilians. The U.S. Pacific Fleet had been all but destroyed with 21 ships, including all 8 battleships, sunk or damaged. At the airfields, only 71 of almost 400 airplanes remained unharmed.

Battleship Row in the aftermath of the attack

Reaction

Immediately after the attack, **medics** rushed to save the 1,143 people who had been injured. Schools, airplane hangars, and lawns were turned into emergency hospitals. It took days to treat all the wounded. Back in Washington, military chiefs said Admiral Kimmel was not prepared and had crowded the U.S. ships too close together, which made them an easy target. Kimmel was fired.

BLACK SAILORS

Many Black American sailors were killed in the attack. They had not received the same combat training as white servicemen because of **segregation** in the U.S. Navy. They were often given low-level jobs onboard ships and had not been trained to fire guns.

The surprise attack on Pearl Harbor outraged Americans and helped rally support for the war.

REMEMBER DEC. 7th!

To War!

The attack on Pearl Harbor pushed the United States to join World War II. On December 8, 1941, Congress declared war on Japan. The United States joined the **Allied powers**. They fought alongside Great Britain, France, and the Soviet Union. The course of World War II changed in an instant.

American military members celebrated when the devastating war ended.

A Devastating War

While war raged in Europe, the U.S. Navy rebuilt its Pacific Fleet. Along with aircraft carriers that had escaped the attack on Pearl Harbor, the new fleet carried U.S. forces to islands across the Pacific, within striking distance of Japan. Officially, the war in Europe ended when Germany surrendered on May 8, 1945. However, Japan fought on until U.S. bombers dropped atomic bombs on two Japanese cities in August 1945, forcing it to surrender just days later.

A TERRIBLE DEATH TOLL

Historians think between 50 million and 70 million people died in World War II, including 400,000 Americans. When the United States dropped atomic bombs on Japan in 1945, at least 215,000 people were killed instantly, with many more dying in the days, weeks, and months that would follow.

KEY DATES

1939

September World War II begins in Europe after Nazi Germany invades Poland.

1940

June Japan invades Indochina. The U.S. Pacific Fleet moves from California to Hawaii.

1941

November Japan moves its aircraft carriers close to Hawaii.

December 2 Emperor Hirohito approves the attack on Pearl Harbor.

December 7

6:05 a.m. Japanese commander Mitsuo Fuchida orders his warplanes into the air

6:45 a.m. The patrol boat USS *Ward* fires the first U.S. shots of the war.

7:49 a.m. Fuchida gives the order to attack.

7:55 a.m. Japanese planes bomb Pearl Harbor and U.S. airfields.

8:00 a.m. Admiral Husband E. Kimmel radios U.S. forces that they are under attack.

8:05 a.m. USS *Oklahoma* is hit and sinks, killing more than 400 people.

8:10 a.m. USS *Arizona* sinks, with the loss of 1,177 people.

9:45 a.m. The attack ends.

December 8 The United States declares war on Japan and enters World War II.

QUIZ   How much have you learned about the attack on Pearl Harbor? It's time to test your knowledge! Then, check your answers on page 32.

1. **What was the day of the week when Japan attacked Pearl Harbor?**
   a) Thursday
   b) Sunday
   c) Tuesday

2. **How long did the attack on Pearl Harbor last?**
   a) a week
   b) 10 minutes
   c) two hours

3. **Which ship was sunk with the loss of over a thousand lives?**
   a) USS *Arizona*
   b) USS *Utah*
   c) USS *Oklahoma*

4. **What were the Japanese attacks targeting?**
   a) a naval base
   b) airfields
   c) both

5. **How did the United States react?**
   a) it did nothing
   b) it declared war on Japan the next day
   c) it bombed Tokyo

GLOSSARY

aircraft carriers large ships with flat decks where planes can take off and land

Allied powers the forces of Great Britain, France, the Soviet Union, and the United States fighting together in World War II

armor strong metal protection for ships, tanks, and other vehicles of war

Axis powers the forces of Japan, Germany, and Italy fighting together in World War II

battleships heavily armed warships

civilians people who are not members of the military

diplomats people who work to keep good relationships between the governments of different countries

expansion the act of becoming larger

gunpowder a black powder that explodes easily

hull the outer shell of a ship

medics people who offer medical care, including on the battlefield

pact a formal agreement between countries or individuals

patrol boat a small, fast warship that is used to watch for enemy activity

personnel military workers

radar a device that uses radio waves to locate and track objects that are far away

resources things that are useful or valuable

segregation the practice of separating people by groups, especially by race

submarines ships that travel underwater

torpedo a long bomb that travels through water

INDEX

aircraft carriers 10, 12, 15, 29

airfields 16–17, 21, 24, 26

Battleship Row 17–18, 26

battleships 4, 15–18, 20–22, 26

Congress, U.S. 5, 28

Fuchida, Mitsuo 12, 15–16

Germany 5, 7–8, 28–29

Hirohito, Emperor 9, 11

Indochina 7–8, 11

Italy 5, 8, 28

Kimmel, Admiral Husband E. 17–18, 27

Miller, Dorie 24

Pacific Fleet, U.S. 4, 8–9, 15, 17, 22, 26–27, 29

pilots 15, 17, 21, 24, 26

radar 14

Roosevelt, President Franklin D. 5, 8–9, 11, 28

submarines 10, 13

warning 14

Yamamoto, Admiral Isoroku 9–10

READ MORE

Bodden, Valerie. *The Attack on Pearl Harbor* (*Disasters for All Time*). Mankato, MN: Creative Education, 2019.

Fowler, Natalie. *A Pearl Harbor Time Capsule: Artifacts of the Surprise Attack on the U.S.* (*Time Capsule History*). North Mankato, MN: Capstone Press, 2021.

Serrano, Christy. *The Attack on Pearl Harbor: A Day That Changed America* (*Days That Changed America*). North Mankato, MN: Capstone Press, 2022.

LEARN MORE ONLINE

1. Go to **www.factsurfer.com** or scan the QR code below.

2. Enter **"Surprise Attack"** into the search box.

3. Click on the cover of this book to see a list of websites.

Answers to the quiz on page 30

1) B; 2) C; 3) A; 4) C; 5) B